Congressional Research Service

Informing the legislative debate since 1914

The Child Tax Credit: Current Law and Legislative History

Margot L. Crandall-Hollick
Analyst in Public Finance

July 28, 2014

Congressional Research Service

7-5700

www.crs.gov

R41873

Summary

This report provides an overview of the child tax credit under current law, as well as a legislative history of this tax benefit, which helps explain its purpose and current structure.

When calculating the total amount of federal income taxes owed, eligible taxpayers can reduce their federal income tax liability by the amount of the child tax credit. Currently, eligible families that claim the child tax credit can subtract up to $1,000 per qualifying child from their federal income tax liability. The maximum amount of credit a family can receive is equal to the number of qualifying children in a family times $1,000. If a family's tax liability is less than the value of their child tax credit, they may be eligible for a refundable credit calculated using the earned income formula. Under this formula, a family is eligible for a refund equal to 15% of their earnings in excess of $3,000, up to the maximum amount of the credit. (This $3,000 amount is referred to as the "refundability threshold.") The credit phases out for single parents with income over $75,000 and married couples with income over $110,000.

The child tax credit was created in 1997 by the Taxpayer Relief Act of 1997 (P.L. 105-34) to help ease the financial burden that families incur when they have children. Like other tax credits, the child tax credit reduces tax liability dollar for dollar of the value of the credit. Initially the child tax credit was a nonrefundable credit for most families. A nonrefundable tax credit can only reduce a taxpayer's tax liability to zero, while a refundable tax credit can exceed a taxpayer's tax liability, providing a cash payment to low-income taxpayers who owe little or no tax.

Since it was first enacted, the child tax credit has undergone significant changes, most notably as a result of the Economic Growth and Tax Relief Reconciliation Act of 2001 (EGTRRA; P.L. 107-16) and the American Recovery and Reinvestment Act of 2009 (ARRA; P.L. 111-5), which increased the availability of the credit to many low-income families. Specifically EGTRRA doubled the value of the credit per child (from $500 to $1,000) and made the credit refundable for families with earnings over $10,000. ARRA lowered this refundability threshold from $10,000 (adjusted annually for inflation) to $3,000 (not adjusted for inflation). As a result of these changes, certain low-income taxpayers are currently eligible for the tax credit if their earnings are greater than $3,000. They receive 15 cents of credit for every dollar of earnings above $3,000 up to the maximum value of the credit—$1,000 per child.

The changes made by EGTRRA and ARRA were extended through the end of 2012 by the Tax Relief, Unemployment Insurance Reauthorization, and Job Creation Act of 2010 (P.L. 111-312). At the end of 2012, the EGTRRA changes to the child tax credit were made permanent, while the ARRA changes were extended for five years (through the end of 2017) as part of the American Taxpayer Relief Act (P.L. 112-240; ATRA). Hence, under current law, beginning in 2018, the child tax credit will still be worth $1,000 per child credit, but the refundability threshold will increase from $3,000 (not adjusted for inflation) to $10,000 (adjusted for inflation occurring after 2001).

In the 113th Congress, several bills have been introduced that would expand the child tax credit for certain taxpayers, including H.R. 769, H.R. 4044, H.R. 4935, S. 836, S. 1616, Chairman Camp's tax reform proposal, and the President's FY2015 budget proposal. Other legislation would modify the taxpayer identification number requirements of either the taxpayer or the child in order to claim the credit, including H.R. 556, H.R. 1674, H.R. 2778, H.R. 3788, H.R. 3885, S. 18, S. 91, S. 1869, S. 1977, and S.Amdt. 2732 to S. 1963.

Contents

Figures

Tables

Appendixes

Contacts

Introduction

The child tax credit was created in 1997 by the Taxpayer Relief Act of 1997 (P.L. 105-34) to help ease the financial burden that families incur when they have children. Like other tax credits, the child tax credit reduces tax liability dollar for dollar of the value of the credit. Initially the child tax credit was a nonrefundable credit for most families. A nonrefundable tax credit can only reduce a taxpayer's tax liability to zero, while a refundable tax credit can exceed a taxpayer's tax liability, providing a cash payment primarily to low-income taxpayers who owe little or no income tax. Over the past 15 years, legislative changes have significantly changed the credit, transforming it from a nonrefundable credit available only to the middle and upper-middle class, to a partially refundable credit that more low-income families are eligible to claim.

As a result of the American Taxpayer Relief Act (P.L. 112-240; ATRA), the child tax credit is permanently refundable. However, at the end of 2017, the earnings threshold at which low-income taxpayers may begin to claim the credit—the "refundability threshold"—is scheduled to rise from $3,000 (not adjusted for inflation) to $10,000 (adjusted for inflation occurring since 2001). Hence, beginning in 2018, under current law, taxpayers with earnings over $10,000 will become eligible for the child tax credit. Currently taxpayers with earnings above $3,000 are eligible for the credit. When the refundability threshold rises, fewer lower income taxpayers will be eligible for the refundable portion of the credit and certain low-income taxpayers will receive a smaller credit.

Prior to the end of 2017, Congress may allow the current policy structure of the credit to expire as scheduled (i.e., allow the refundability threshold to increase), they may extend current policy (i.e., keep the refundability threshold at $3,000 either temporarily or permanently), or they may modify different parameters of the credit. This report provides an overview of the credit under current law and examines the legislative history of the credit, reviewing how the credit has changed over the past two decades to provide background to any upcoming debate on the future of this tax benefit. This report also includes a brief overview of selected legislation introduced in the 113th Congress that would modify the child tax credit.[1] For an economic analysis of the child tax credit, see CRS Report R41935, *The Child Tax Credit: Economic Analysis and Policy Options*, by Margot L. Crandall-Hollick.

Current Law

Currently, the child tax credit allows a taxpayer to reduce their federal income tax liability (the taxes owed before tax credits are applied) by up to $1,000 per child. If the value of the credit exceeds the amount of tax a family owes, the family may be eligible to receive a full or partial refund of the difference.[2] The total amount of their refund is calculated as 15% (the refundability rate) of earnings that exceed $3,000 (the refundability threshold), up to the maximum amount of the credit ($1,000 per child). The credit phases out for higher-income taxpayers. The child tax credit can offset a taxpayer's Alternative Minimum Tax (AMT) liability. One parameter of the

---

[1] The legislation summarized in this report includes a broad variety of bills that expand the credit by adjusting various parameters of the credit or change the taxpayer identification requirements of the credit. It also includes major proposals that have been evaluated by the Joint Committee on Taxation or the Treasury Department.

[2] The refundable portion of the credit is sometimes referred to as the "additional child tax credit" or ACTC.

child tax credit is scheduled to expire at the end of 2017, namely the refundability threshold. Currently, the maximum credit per child, refundability threshold, and phase-out thresholds are not indexed for inflation. **Table 1** provides an overview of key provisions of the child tax credit under current law for tax years 2009-2017, and beyond.

Table 1. Overview of Key Aspects of the Child Tax Credit Under Current Law

Parameter	Through 2017	After 2017
Maximum credit per child	$1,000	same
Refundability Threshold	$3,000	$10,000 (indexed for inflation occurring since 2001)[a]
Refundability Rate	15%	same
Phase-Out Threshold	$55,000 married separate return $75,000 unmarried taxpayer $110,000 married joint return	same
Phase-Out Rate	5%	same
Offset AMT tax liability	YES	same

Source: Internal Revenue Code, 26 U.S.C. §24.

a. JCT estimated the $10,000 refundability threshold adjusted for inflation would equal $13,600 in 2014. For more information, see Joint Committee on Taxation, Technical Explanation of the Tax Reform Act of 2014, February 26, 2014, JCX-12-14 at https://www.jct.gov/publications.html.

Detailed Overview of Current Credit

Given legislative interest in modifying the child tax credit, as well as the scheduled increase of the current refundability threshold at the end of 2017, each of the key parameters of the child tax credit are described. In addition, a brief overview of how modification of the parameter would affect the credit value is provided.

Maximum Credit per Child

Eligible families can claim a child tax credit and reduce their federal income tax liability by up to $1,000 per qualifying child.[3] The maximum credit a family can receive is equal to the number of qualifying children a taxpayer has, multiplied by $1,000. For example, a family with two qualifying children may be eligible for a $2,000 credit. Families may receive the child tax credit as a reduction in tax liability (the non-refundable portion of the credit), a refundable credit, or a combination of both.[4] For example, a family with two qualifying children and a tax liability of $1,500 may receive the $2,000 child tax credit as a $1,500 reduction in their tax liability and a $500 refund.[5]

---

[3] The child tax credit can be found in Section 24 of the Internal Revenue Code (26 U.S.C. §24).

[4] Importantly, even if the credit both reduces tax liability and then is received as a refund, the total value of the non-refundable and refundable portion of the credit cannot exceed $1,000 per child multiplied by the number of qualifying children. Hence, if a family with two children and a $1,500 tax liability is eligible for a $2,000 child tax credit, $1,500 of their credit will reduce their tax liability to zero (the non-refundable portion) and the family may recover up to $500 of child tax credit as a refundable credit, depending on their income.

[5] The family will need earnings of at least $8,335 to receive a refundable child tax credit of $500. If their earnings are (continued...)

All else being unchanged from current law, increasing the maximum credit per child would result in a larger credit for middle- and upper-income families who currently receive the credit, while certain lower-income families would see their credit value unchanged, as illustrated in the top portion of **Figure 1**.[6] In **Figure 1** (and all subsequent figures in this report) an increase in the credit corresponds to a positive change in the credit amount; a decrease corresponds to a negative change in the credit amount, while no change corresponds to zero. (For illustrative purposes only, the maximum credit per child is either increased to $2,000 (blue) or reduced to $500 (red) in comparison with the current law level of $1,000 in **Figure 1**.) Conversely, as illustrated in the bottom portion of **Figure 1**, reducing the size of the maximum credit per child would reduce the credit value for certain low-income families, as well as middle- and upper-income families, while some of the lowest-income families' credits would remain unchanged. Among these unaffected taxpayers, many already receive *less than the maximum* child tax credit under current law (and in some cases, no credit). Hence *changes to the maximum value* of the credit would not affect them.

Figure 1. The Change in the Child Tax Credit from Increasing or Decreasing the Maximum Credit per Child, by Earnings

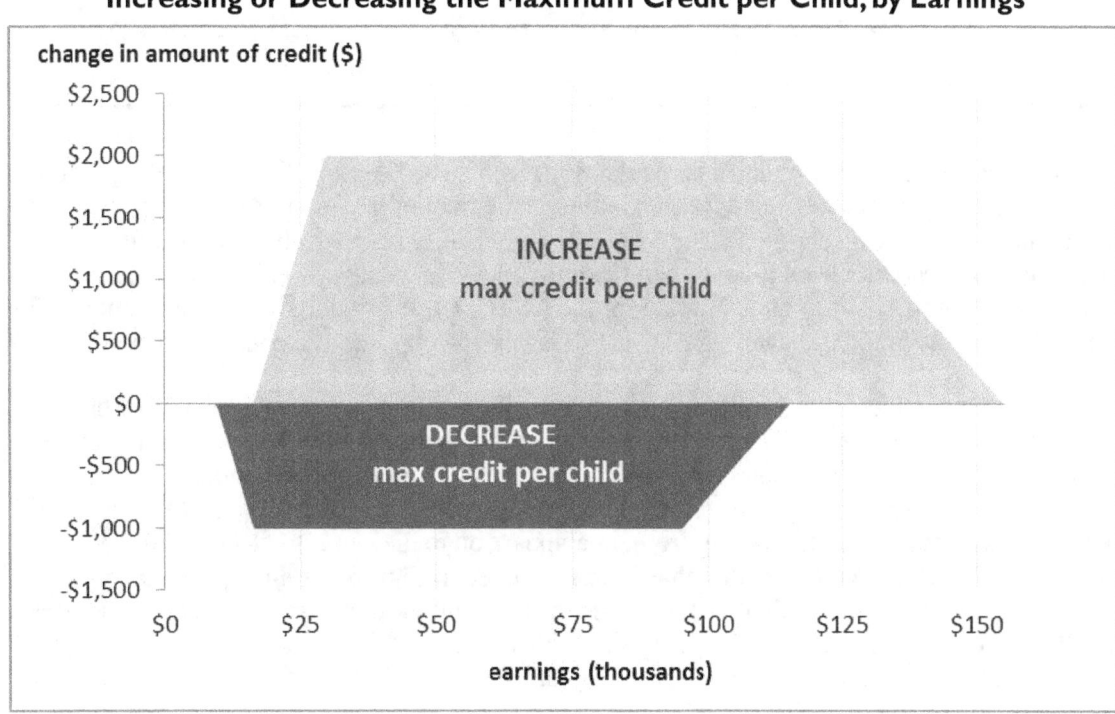

Source: Congressional Research Service.

The Refundability Threshold and Refundability Rate

For taxpayers with little or no federal income tax liability, they will be eligible for little if any of the non-refundable portion of the child tax credit. Instead, they may be eligible to receive the

---

(...continued)

less, their refundable child tax credit will be less than $500 and the total value of the credit (refundable plus non-refundable portion) will be less than $2,000.

[6] For **Figure 1** through **Figure 5**, it is assumed that all income is from earnings; that the taxpayer is an unmarried, single parent with two children; and that she files her taxes using head-of-household status.

child tax credit as a refundable credit. The refundable portion of the child tax credit is often referred to as the additional child tax credit or ACTC. The amount of the refundable child tax credit is generally calculated using the "earned income formula."[7]

The Earned Income Formula

Earned Income Formula

(earnings - refundability threshold) x (refundability rate)

The total amount of the child tax credit calculated under the earned income formula cannot exceed the maximum allowable credit. The maximum value of the credit is $1,000 credit per child multiplied by the number of qualifying children

Example

Two-parent, three-child family with earnings of $20,000

($20,000 - $3,000) x 15%= $2,550

Note that in this example $2,550 does not exceed the maximum value of the credit which is $3,000 (3 times $1,000 per child).

Under the earned income formula, a taxpayer may claim an ACTC equal to 15% of the family's earnings in excess of $3,000, up to the maximum credit amount (i.e., up to $1,000 multiplied by the number of qualifying children). The $3,000 amount is referred to as the refundability threshold; the 15% is referred to as the refundability rate. If a taxpayer's earnings are below the refundability threshold, they are ineligible for the ACTC. For every dollar of earnings above this amount, the value of the taxpayer's ACTC increases by 15 cents, up to the maximum amount.

If all the other parameters of the child tax credit remain the same, increasing the refundability threshold reduces the size of the credit for the lowest-income families, while middle- and upper-income families will not see their credit value change, as illustrated in the bottom portion of **Figure 2**. (For illustrative purposes only, the refundability threshold is either decreased to zero dollars (blue) or increased to $14,650 (red), in comparison to the current level of $3,000 in **Figure 2**.) The $14,650 refundability threshold illustrated in **Figure 2** is an approximation of what the refundability threshold may be in 2018, when the threshold is scheduled to revert back to $10,000 adjusted for inflation occurring since 2001.[8] Conversely, as illustrated in the top portion of **Figure 2**, decreasing the refundability threshold would increase the value of the credit

---

[7] Families with three or more children may choose to calculate the refundable portion of the child tax credit using an alternative formula. If the amount calculated under the alternative formula is larger than the refundable credit calculated under the earned income formula, the larger credit can be claimed. The alternative formula is calculated as the excess of a taxpayer's payroll taxes (including one-half of any self-employment taxes) over their earned income tax credit (EITC), not to exceed the maximum credit amount. However, lower-income taxpayers will often pay less in payroll taxes than they will receive in the EITC. This is because payroll taxes are equal to 7.65% of earnings, while the EITC equals up to 45% of earnings.

[8] Under current law, beginning in 2018, the $10,000 inflation adjustment will be calculated by multiplying this amount by the consumer price index (CPI) in 2017 by the CPI in 2000. Projections of the CPI in 2017 came from the Congressional Budget Office (http://cbo.gov/publication/45010, see "Date Underlying Figures"). Since this inflation adjusted amount was an approximation, and given data limitations, the annual calendar year average inflation levels for 2017 and 2000 were used. In actuality, the statute states the CPI for any calendar year is the average of the Consumer Price Index as of the close of the 12-month period ending on August 31 of such calendar year. So the CPI for 2017 would be equal to the annual average of the CPI from September 2016 to August 2017.

for the lowest-income taxpayers, while the value of the credit for middle- and upper-income taxpayers would remain unchanged. Some of the taxpayers who would benefit from reducing the refundability threshold would be newly eligible, while others already receiving the credit would receive a larger credit since more of their earnings would be used in calculating its value under the earned income formula.

Figure 2. The Change in the Child Tax Credit from Increasing or Decreasing the Refundability Threshold, by Earnings

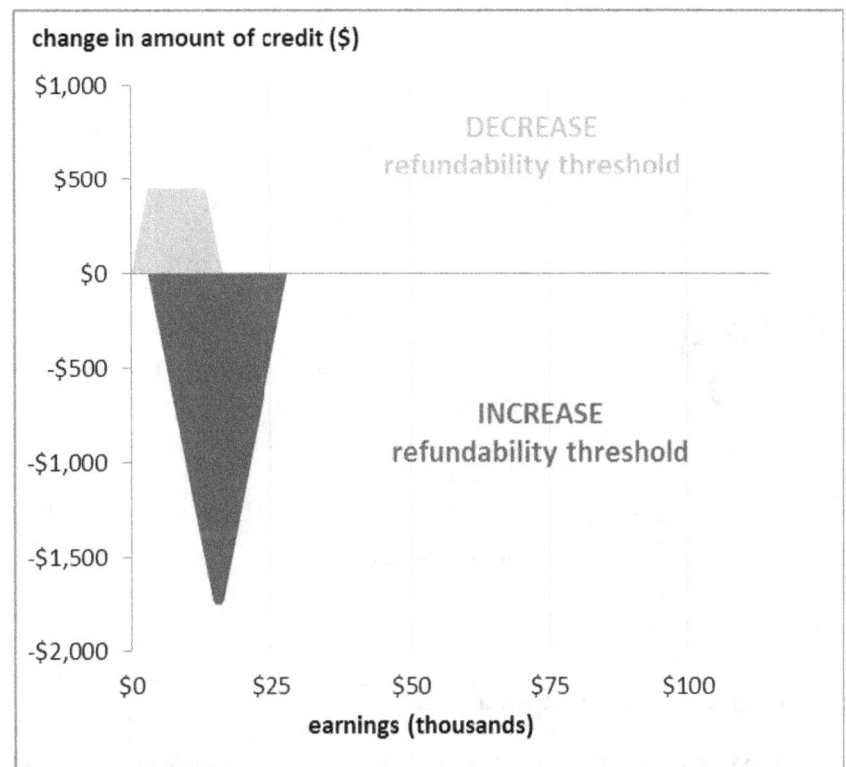

Source: Congressional Research Service.

Changing the other parameter of the earned income formula—the refundability rate—would also change the value of the credit for certain taxpayers. All else being unchanged from current law, increasing the refundability rate would increase the value of the credit for the lowest-income taxpayers if their earnings exceeded the refundability threshold, while the value of the credit for middle- and upper-income taxpayers would remain unchanged as illustrated in the top portion of **Figure 3**. (For illustrative purposes only, the refundability rate is either decreased to 10% (red) or increased to 50% (blue), in comparison to the current level of 15% in **Figure 3**.) Conversely, as illustrated in the bottom portion of **Figure 3**, decreasing the refundability rate would reduce the size of the credit for certain lower-income families and middle-income families (as long as their income is greater than the refundability threshold), while other middle- and upper-income families would not see their credit value change.[9] Notably, the poorest taxpayers, those with

---

[9] As the refundability rate decreases further, the actual impact on the credit amount for middle-income taxpayers will depend on their particular circumstances. For some taxpayers, the refundable portion of the credit will fall, but if they have income tax liability, they may also receive the non-refundable portion of the credit as well. Hence, the total value of the credit may ultimately remain unchanged.

income below the refundability threshold, would not see their credit value change if only the refundability rate were to be increased.

Figure 3. The Change in the Child Tax Credit from Increasing or Decreasing the Refundability Rate, by Earnings

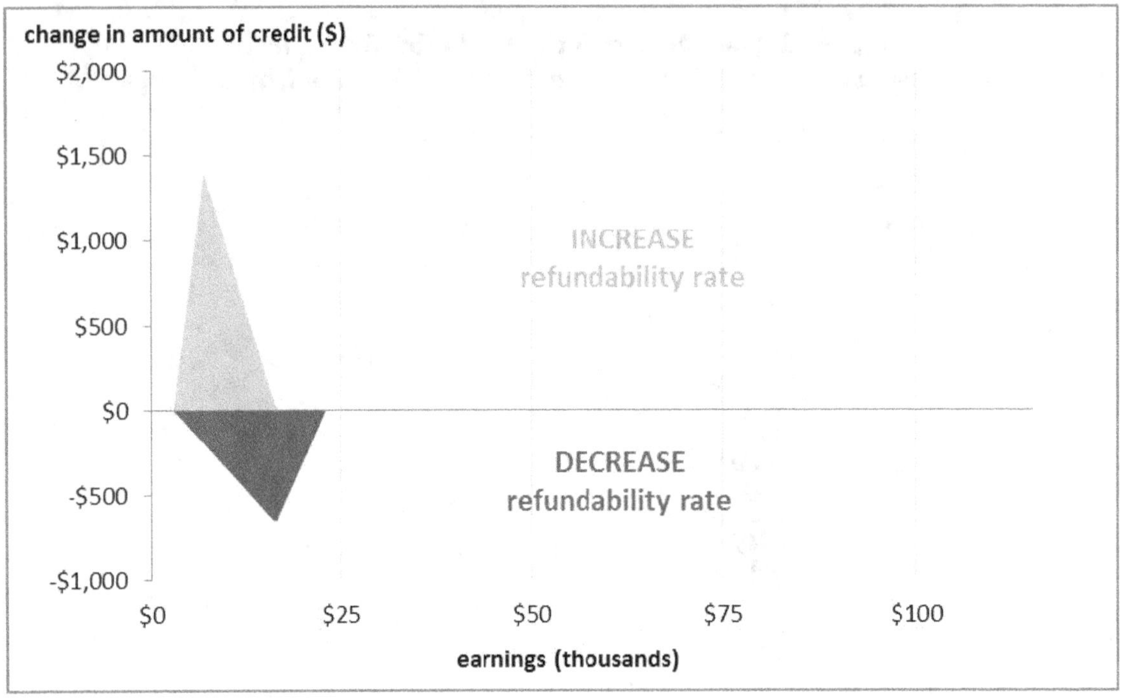

Source: Congressional Research Service.

The Phase-Out Threshold and Phase-Out Rate

The child tax credit phases out for higher-income families. The $1,000-per-child value of the credit falls by a certain amount as a family's income rises. Specifically, for every $1,000 of modified adjusted gross income (MAGI)[10] above a threshold amount, the credit falls by $50—or effectively by 5% of MAGI above the threshold. The threshold amounts depend on a taxpayer's filing status, and equal $75,000 for single parents, $110,000 for married taxpayers filing joint returns, and $55,000 for married taxpayers filing separate returns. The actual income level at which the credit is entirely phased out depends on the number of qualifying children a taxpayer has. Generally, it takes $20,000 of MAGI above the phase-out threshold to completely phase out $1,000 of credit. For example, the credit will completely phase out for a married couple with two children if their MAGI exceeds $150,000.

All else being unchanged from current law, increasing the phase-out threshold would increase the value of the credit for middle- and upper-income taxpayers, while the credit amount for lower-

---

[10] With respect to the child tax credit, modified adjusted gross income (MAGI) is equal to Adjusted Gross Income (AGI) increased by foreign earned income of U.S. Citizens abroad, including income earned in Guam, American Samoa, the Northern Mariana Islands, and Puerto Rico. For more information on AGI see CRS Report RL30110, *Federal Individual Income Tax Terms: An Explanation*, by Mark P. Keightley and Jeffrey M. Stupak; and CRS Report RL32808, *Overview of the Federal Tax System*, by Molly F. Sherlock and Donald J. Marples.

income taxpayers would remain unchanged as illustrated in the top portion of **Figure 4**. Specifically, many taxpayers whose income currently exceeds the phase-out threshold would receive a larger credit. (For illustrative purposes only, the phase-out threshold is either increased to $100,000 (blue) or reduced to $50,000 (red) for an unmarried taxpayer, in comparison to the current level of $75,000 in **Figure 4**.) Conversely, as shown in the bottom portion of **Figure 4**, decreasing the phase-out threshold would reduce the value of the credit for middle- and upper-income taxpayers, who would see their credit begin to phase out at lower income levels than under current law.

Figure 4. The Change in the Child Tax Credit from Increasing or Decreasing the Phase-Out Threshold, by Earnings

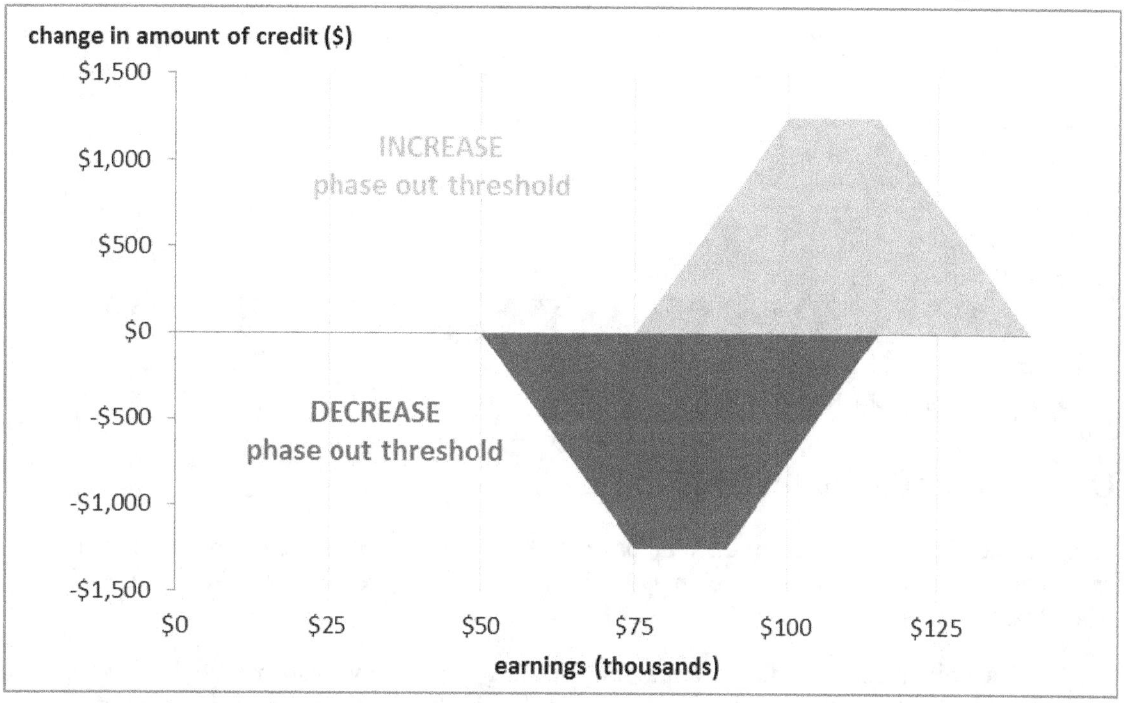

Source: Congressional Research Service.

With respect to the phase-out rate, changing the rate that the credit phases out would change the amount of the credit for taxpayers whose income is greater than the phase-out threshold. These taxpayers already experience a reduction in the credit based on their income level (i.e., they are in the "phase-out range" of the credit). Increasing the phase-out rate would decrease the value of the credit for middle- and upper-income taxpayers in the phase-out range, as illustrated in the bottom portion of **Figure 5**. (For illustrative purposes only, the phase-out rate is either increased to 20% (blue) or reduced to 1% (red), in comparison to the current level of 5% in **Figure 5**.) Conversely, as illustrated in the top portion of **Figure 5**, decreasing the phase-out rate would increase the value of the credit for middle- and upper-income taxpayers whose income currently places them in the phase-out range of the credit. Those taxpayers whose income is below the phase-out threshold would be unaffected by changes to the phase-out rate.

Figure 5. The Change in the Child Tax Credit from Increasing or Decreasing the Phase-Out Rate, by Earnings

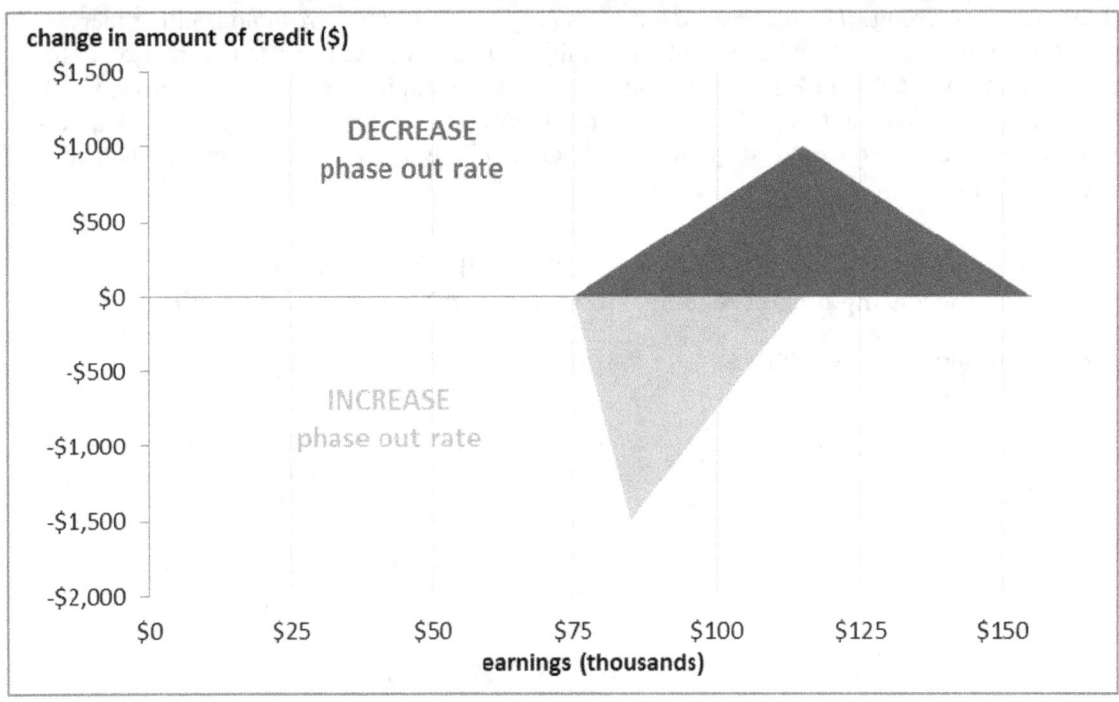

Source: Congressional Research Service.

Definition of a Qualifying Child

In order to claim the child tax credit, a taxpayer's child must be considered "a qualifying child" and meet several requirements which may differ from eligibility requirements for other child-related tax benefits:[11]

1. The child must be under 17 years of age during the entire year for which the taxpayer claims the credit (for example, if the child was 16.5 years on December 31, 2010, the taxpayer could claim the credit on their 2010 federal income tax return).

2. The child must be claimed as a dependent on the taxpayer's return.

3. The child must be the taxpayer's son, daughter, grandson, granddaughter, stepson, stepdaughter, niece, nephew, or an eligible foster child of the taxpayer.

4. The child must live at the same principal residence as the taxpayer for more than half the year for which the taxpayer wishes to claim in the credit.

5. The child cannot provide more than half of their own support during the tax year.

6. The child must be a U.S. citizen. If they are not a U.S. citizen, they must be a resident of the United States. The statute requires that taxpayers who intend to claim the child tax credit provide a valid Taxpayer Identification Number (TIN)

---

[11] For more information on what a qualifying child is for the child tax credit in comparison to other child-related tax benefits, see CRS Report RS22016, *Tax Benefits for Families: Changes in the Definition of a Child*, by Christine Scott.

for each qualifying child on their federal income tax return. In most cases, this
TIN will be the child's Social Security number.

The age and citizenship requirements for a qualifying child for the child tax credit differ from the definition of qualifying child used for other tax benefits and can cause confusion among taxpayers. For example, a taxpayer's 18-year-old child may meet all the requirements for a qualifying child for the EITC, but will be too old to be eligible for the child tax credit.

Recent Legislative History

The child tax credit was initially structured in the Taxpayer Relief Act of 1997 (P.L. 105-34) as a $500-per-child nonrefundable credit to provide tax relief to middle- and upper-middle-income families. Since 1997, various laws have modified key parameters of the credit, expanding the availability of the benefit to more low-income families while also increasing the value of the tax credit. The first significant change to the child tax credit occurred with the enactment of the Economic Growth and Tax Relief Reconciliation Act of 2001 (EGTRRA; P.L. 107-16). EGTRRA increased the amount of the credit over time to $1,000 per child and made it partially refundable under the earned income formula. For more information on the exact parameter changes, see **Table 2**. Subsequent legislation enacted in 2003 and 2004 accelerated the implementation of the changes made under EGTRRA. In 2008 and 2009, Congress enacted legislation, the Emergency Economic Stabilization Act of 2009 (EESA; P.L. 110-343) and the American Recovery and Reinvestment Act of 2009 (ARRA; P.L. 111-5), which further expanded the availability and amount of the credit to taxpayers whose income was too low to either qualify for the credit or be eligible for the full credit. EESA lowered the refundability threshold to $8,500 in 2008, while ARRA lowered the refundability threshold to $3,000 for 2009 through 2010. The Tax Relief, Unemployment Insurance Reauthorization, and Job Creation Act of 2010 (P.L. 111-312) extended both the EGTRRA provisions of the child tax credit and the expansion of refundability under ARRA for two years through the end of 2012.

ATRA made all of the EGTRRA modifications to the child tax credit permanent and extended the ARRA modifications for five years, through the end of 2017. Hence, the child tax credit is (absent legislative changes) permanently $1,000 per child. The credit is also permanently partially refundable using the earned income formula whereby the refundable portion of the credit equals 15% of earnings in excess of the refundability threshold. Under ATRA, the refundability threshold is equal to $3,000 from 2013 to 2017 (not indexed for inflation), and is scheduled to rise to $10,000 (indexed for inflation occurring since 2001) in 2018.

Table 2. Changes to the Child Tax Credit Made by Legislation 1997-2013

Parameter	1997 P.L. 105-34	1999 P.L. 106-170	2001 P.L. 107-16 (EGTRRA)	2003 P.L. 108-27 (JGTRRA)	2004 P.L. 108-311 (WFTRA)	2008 P.L. 110-343 (EESA)	2009 P.L. 111-5 (ARRA)	2010 P.L. 111-312	2013 P.L. 112-240 (ATRA)
Maximum Credit per Child	$400 (1998) $500 (after)	*	$600 (2001-04) $700 (2005-08) $800 (2009) $1,000 (2010)	$1,000 (2003-04)	$1,000 (2005-10)	*	*	$1,000 (2011-12)	$1,000 (permanent)
Inflation adj.	NO	*	*	*	*	*	*	*	*
Refundable[a]	NO	*	YES (2001-2010)	*	*	*	*	YES (2011-2012)	YES (permanent)
Refundability Threshold	na	*	$10,000 (2001-10)	*	*	$8,500 (2008)	$3,000 (2009-10)	$3,000 (2011-12)	$3,000 (2013-2017) $10,000
Inflation Adj.	na	*	YES (2002-10)	*	*	NO	NO (2009-2010)	NO (2011-12)	NO (2013-2017) YES therafter
Refundability Rate	na	*	10% (2001-04) 15% (2005-10)	*	15% (2004-2010)	*	*	15% (2011-12)	15% (permanent)
Phase-Out Threshold[b]	$55,000 MFS $75,000 HOH $110,00 MFJ	*	*	*	*	*	*	*	*
Phase-Out Rate	5%	*	*	*	*	*	*	*	*
Offset AMT	NO	YES (2000-01)	YES (2002-10)	*	*	*	*	YES (2011-2012)	YES (permanent)
Revenue Effect	-$183.38 billion (1997-07)	-$2.89 billion[c] (2000-09)	-$171.78 billion (2001-11)	-$32.49 billion (2003-13)	-$63.77 billion (2005-14)	-$3.13 billion (2009-18)	-$14.83 billion (2009-19)	-$91.44 billion (2011-20)	-$405.01 billion (2013-2022)

Source: Joint Committee on Taxation

Notes: *-Indicates unchanged from prior law. Except as otherwise noted, revenue effects reflect the cost of the child tax credit provisions exclusively.

a. Prior to EGTRRA, the child credit was only refundable for families with three or more children under the alternative formula.

b. MFS, HOH, and MFJ refer to tax filing status, specifically: MFS: married filing separately; HOH: head of household; MFJ: married filing joint.

c. This law allowed nonrefundable personal credits (including the child tax credit) to offset the tentative minimum tax) for tax year 1999 (which was an extension of a provision in P.L. 105-277). For tax years 2000 and 2001, this law included a special provision that allowed personal nonrefundable credits in full against regular tax and the AMT. The revenue effect reflects the effect of these provisions on personal nonrefundable credit, and is not limited to their effect on the child tax credit.

EGTRRA, JGTRRA, and WFTRA

The Economic Growth and Tax Relief Reconciliation Act of 2001 (EGTRRA; P.L. 107-16) made four significant changes to the child tax credit. First, EGTRRA increased the maximum amount of the credit per child in scheduled increments until it reached $1,000 per child in 2010. Second, EGTRRA made the credit refundable for families irrespective of size using the earned income formula. For tax years 2001 through 2004, the earned income formula set the amount of the refundable portion of the credit equal to 10% of a taxpayer's earned income in excess of $10,000, up to the maximum amount of the credit for that tax year. The refundability rate was scheduled to increase to 15% for tax years 2005 through 2010. The $10,000 threshold was indexed for inflation beginning in 2002. Third, EGTRRA allowed the child tax credit to offset AMT tax liability for tax years 2002 through 2010. Fourth, the law temporarily repealed the prior law provision that reduced the refundable portion of the child tax credit by the amount of the AMT. All the EGTRRA provisions were scheduled to expire at the end of 2010.

The Jobs Growth and Tax Relief Reconciliation Act of 2003 (JGTRRA; P.L. 108-27) temporarily accelerated the scheduled increase in the maximum credit amount. Specifically, while EGTRRA increased the maximum credit amount to $600 per child for 2003 and 2004, JGTRRA increased this amount to $1,000 per child for those two years. In the summer of 2003, the $400 increase in the credit for 2003 was paid in advance from the Treasury Department to many families who qualified for the child tax credit. These direct payments were distributed based on information contained on taxpayers' 2002 income tax returns. The JGTRRA provisions were scheduled to expire after 2004, and the child tax credit would have reverted to its scheduled level under EGTRRA—$700 per child in 2005.

In September 2004, Congress passed the Working Families Tax Relief Act of 2004 (WFTRA; P.L. 108-311), which further accelerated the implementation of key provisions of EGTRRA. This act extended the maximum amount of the credit established under JGTRRA, $1,000 per child, through 2009. For 2010, the EGTRRA provisions would apply and the maximum amount of the credit would remain $1,000 per child. In addition, WFTRA increased the refundability rate to 15% for 2004. Under EGTRRA, the refundability rate would remain at 15% from 2005 through 2010.

WFTRA also contained a provision that allowed combat pay to be included as part of earned income for purposes of computing refundability of the child tax credit. As more soldiers began to see combat due to the wars in Iraq and Afghanistan, they started receiving combat pay. Income earned by members of the armed services in a combat zone is generally excluded from taxation. This exclusion benefits taxpayers who have positive tax liability and reduces the taxes they owe. However, for some lower-income members of the Armed Forces, the exclusion resulted in earnings being too low to qualify for the refundable portion of the child tax credit. The inclusion of combat pay as earned income for purposes of calculating the refundable child tax credit under WFTRA meant that the earnings of some military families would increase above the refundability threshold, ultimately resulting in larger child tax credit refunds. This change was for 2004 through 2010, and was scheduled to expire, along with other provisions of EGTRRA, at the end of 2010.

EESA, ARRA, and P.L. 111-312

In October 2008, Congress passed the Emergency Economic Stabilization Act of 2009 (EESA; P.L. 110-343) in response to the financial and housing crisis. The law included a provision to lower the refundability threshold for the child tax credit for 2008 from $12,050[12] to $8,500. In the absence of any additional congressional action, the refundability threshold was scheduled to increase to $12,550 in 2009.

In early 2009, Congress began to debate different legislative proposals for economic stimulus. Part of that debate concerned changing the refundability threshold of the child tax credit. The House proposed[13] reducing the refundability threshold to zero for 2009 and 2010, while the Senate proposed[14] lowering the refundability threshold to $8,100 over the same time period. The House's proposed changes to the child tax credit were estimated to cost $18.3 billion over 10 years, in comparison to $7.2 billion for the Senate proposal. The provision took its final shape during the meetings between the Senate and the House conferees.[15] In February 2009 Congress passed the American Recovery and Reinvestment Act of 2009 (ARRA; P.L. 111-5), which ultimately reduced the refundability threshold to $3,000 for 2009 and 2010. This proposal was estimated to cost $14.8 billion over 10 years.[16]

At the end of 2010, both the EGTRRA and ARRA provisions of the child tax credit (see **Table 2**) were scheduled to expire. Since ARRA's changes to the refundability threshold built upon changes made by EGTRRA, the expiration of EGTRRA would effectively terminate the expansion of refundability made by the 2009 stimulus law (ARRA). Absent an extension of EGTRRA, the maximum amount of the child tax credit would have reverted to $500 per child, the credit would only have been refundable to families with three or more children using the alternative formula, and the amount of the child tax credit would not have been allowed in full against the AMT. In December 2010, Congress passed the Tax Relief, Unemployment Insurance Reauthorization, and Job Creation Act of 2010 (P.L. 111-312), which extended both the EGTRRA provisions of the child tax credit[17] and the expansion of refundability from ARRA for two years through the end of 2012.

ATRA

At the end of 2012, Congress passed the American Taxpayer Relief Act of 2012 (P.L. 112-240; ATRA). This law made the EGTRRA changes to the child tax credit permanent and extended the $3,000 refundability threshold enacted as part of ARRA for five years, through the end of 2017. Hence, the child tax credit is now permanently $1,000 per child, and partially refundable whereby

---

[12] The $10,000 threshold established by EGTRRA, adjusted for inflation.

[13] H.R. 1 that passed the House on January 28, 2009

[14] S.Amdt. 570 in the nature of a substitute to H.R. 1, which passed the Senate on February 10, 2009.

[15] See the Conference Report H.Rept. 111-16.

[16] U.S. Congress, Joint Committee on Taxation, JCX-19-09, *Estimated Budget Effects Of The Revenue Provisions Contained In The Conference Agreement For H.R. 1, The "American Recovery And Reinvestment Tax Act Of 2009,"* February 12, 2009, p. 1.

[17] This includes the inclusion of combat pay as part of earned income for purposes of calculating refundability under the earned income formula created by EGTRRA. In addition this law extended for two years (through the end of 2012) the EGTRRA repeal of a prior-law provision that reduced the refundable portion of the child credit by the amount of the AMT and it extended the EGTRRA provision which allowed the child tax credit to offset a taxpayer's AMT.

---

the refundable portion is equal to 15% of earnings in excess of the refundability threshold. That threshold is temporarily $3,000 between 2013 through 2017, and permanently $10,000 (indexed for inflation occurring after 2001) thereafter. In addition, the child tax credit can permanently offset the AMT as a result of ATRA. **Table 2** summarizes the key changes made to the credit by several pieces of legislation.

Selected Legislation in the 113th Congress that Modifies the Child Tax Credit

In the 113th Congress, there have been a variety of legislative proposals introduced that would modify the child tax credit. Generally, these modifications take one of two forms—legislation that increases the value of the credit for certain taxpayers and legislation that modifies the taxpayer identification requirements of the credit. Legislation which increases the value of the credit is summarized below and outlined in **Table 4**. (Given the variety of changes made to the child tax credit in the context of broader tax reform, a more detailed table outlining the changes made to the child tax credit by the Camp proposal is provided in **Table 3**.) Legislation which modifies the taxpayer ID requirements of the child tax credit is also discussed and summarized in **Table 5**.

The legislation summarized in this report includes a broad variety of bills that expand the credit by adjusting various parameters or changing the taxpayer identification requirements of the credit. Some of these bills have been evaluated by the Joint Committee on Taxation or the Treasury Department. Others reflect policy options that Congress has considered in the recent past.

Legislation that Expands the Child Tax Credit

There are a variety of legislative proposals which have been introduced in the 113th Congress that expand the child tax credit for certain taxpayers. These bills expand the child tax credit in a variety of different ways, including by increasing the phase-out threshold, increasing the amount of maximum credit per child, increasing the refundability rate of the credit, or lowering the refundability threshold. In some cases, the bills modify more than one of these parameters. These bills are summarized below.

Under all but two bills described in this report—H.R. 769 and S. 836—the ARRA expansion to the child tax credit would expire as currently scheduled at the end of 2017. Hence, beginning in 2018, the refundability threshold would increase from its current level of $3,000 to $10,000 (adjusted for inflation occurring since 2001).

H.R. 4935 (Representative Jenkins)

The Child Tax Credit Improvement Act of 2014 (H.R. 4935) introduced by Representative Jenkins would expand the child tax credit in two ways. First, the bill would annually adjust the maximum credit amount per child for inflation.[18] This would likely result in the maximum credit

---

[18] The credit amount would be adjusted for inflation occurring after 2014 and then rounded to the nearest multiple of $50 under this bill.

amount per child gradually increasing in future years. Second, the bill would increase the phase-out threshold for married taxpayers. Specifically, the income level at which the credit begins to phase out for married taxpayers filing joint returns would increase from $110,000 to $150,000. Further, these thresholds would be adjusted annually for inflation, potentially increasing them in subsequent years.[19]

The Joint Committee on Taxation estimates that this bill would reduce revenues by $114.9 billion between 2015 and 2024.[20] Analysis by the Tax Policy Center indicates that taxpayers with income between $100,000 and $200,000 would receive the largest benefit from this proposal.[21] On June 25, 2014, the House Ways and Means Committee reported H.R. 4935 favorably out of committee by a vote of 22 to 15.[22] On July 25, 2014, the House passed H.R. 4935 by a vote of 237-173. (Pursuant to the rule under which the bill was considered, the text of the bill was added as new matter to H.R. 3393.)[23]

H.R. 4044 (Representative Braley)

The Child Tax Credit Restoration Act of 2014 (H.R. 4044), introduced by Representative Braley, would temporarily expand the child tax credit for 2014 and 2015 in two ways, after which the credit would revert to its parameters under current law. First, the bill would increase the maximum credit amount per child from $1,000 to $2,000. Second, it would double the refundability rate to 30%. Beginning in 2016, these changes would expire and the credit amount and refundability rate would revert to $1,000 per child and 15%, respectively.

H.R. 769 (Representative DeLauro) and S. 836 (Senator Brown)

The Child Tax Credit Permanency Act (H.R. 769), introduced by Representative DeLauro, and Section 2 of The Working Families Tax Relief Act (S. 836), introduced by Senator Brown,[24] would both make the ARRA expansion to the child tax credit—the $3,000 refundability threshold—permanent. In addition, both bills would adjust the $1,000 per child credit amount annually for inflation.[25]

---

[19] After adjusting the income phase-out threshold for inflation occurring after 2014, the thresholds would be rounded to the nearest multiple of $1,000 under this bill.

[20] This figure includes an increased outlay for the refundable portion of the credit of $21 billion between 2015 and 2024. For more information, see http://waysandmeans.house.gov/uploadedfiles/ jct_description_of_amendment_in_the_nature_of_a_substitute_to_h r._4935_green_sheet.pdf.

[21] For more information, see http://taxpolicycenter.org/numbers/displayatab.cfm?Docid=4119&DocTypeID=1.

[22] See http://waysandmeans.house.gov/uploadedfiles/h r._4935_final_passage.pdf.

[23] On July 24, 2014, the House agreed to a special rule reported from the House Rules Committee (H.Res. 680) that provided for consideration of H.R. 4935. On July 25, the House considered the bill under a closed rule which meant that no amendments were in order, and then passed H.R. 4935 by a vote of 237-173. Pursuant to the special rule, the text of H.R. 4935 was then added as new matter to the bill H.R. 3393 as passed by the House on July 24, and H.R. 4935 was laid upon the table.

[24] In addition to modifying the child tax credit, this bill also makes modifications to the earned income tax credit (EITC).

[25] Under S. 836, the $1,000 amount would be adjusted for inflation occurring since 2012, while under H.R. 769 the credit amount would be adjusted for inflation occurring after 2013.

S. 1616 (Senator Lee)

Section 4 of the Family Fairness and Opportunity Tax Reform Act (S. 1616),[26] introduced by Senator Lee, would create a new $2,500 per child "additional child tax credit" (hereinafter referred to as the "additional refundable credit for children" or ARCC). This credit would be claimed *in addition to* the current $1,000 child tax credit for a child that meets the eligibility requirements of the current child tax credit. Hence, certain taxpayers could receive a combined credit of $3,500 per child—the current $1,000 per child credit and the $2,500 ARCC. Importantly, none of the parameters of the current child tax credit would change under this bill.

The ARCC would be refundable, but the formula used to calculate the refundable portion of the ARCC would differ from the formula generally used to calculate the refundable portion of the child tax credit. Specifically, the portion of the ARCC that would be refundable would be equal to the amount by which a taxpayer's combined individual income taxes and payroll taxes (both the employer and employee share) exceeded the taxpayer's earned income tax credit (EITC). In other words, the refundable portion of the credit would equal 15.3% of the taxpayers' earnings, minus the value of their EITC, up to the maximum of $2,500 per child. The $2,500 amount would be indexed for inflation after 2013 based on the change in the national average wage index. (In contrast, under current law, the parameters of the child tax credit which are adjusted for inflation are adjusted based on changes in the consumer price index or CPI.) Finally, the $2,500 ARCC would not phase out. Hence taxpayers who are currently ineligible for the child tax credit because their incomes are too high could receive the $2,500 ARCC.

Camp Tax Reform Proposal

On February 26, 2014, Chairman Camp of the House Committee on Ways and Means introduced a draft tax reform bill that, among other things, would modify or repeal a variety of tax benefits for children and families, including the child tax credit. The Camp proposal would increase the size of the child tax credit, expand the credit to non-child dependents, increase the refundability rate, lower the refundability income threshold, and include new limitations on eligibility for the credit for non-citizens.[27] A full description of the key changes made can be found in **Table 3**. The Joint Committee on Taxation estimates these changes would reduce revenues by $554.0 billion between 2014 and 2023.

FY2015 Budget Proposal

The Obama Administration's FY2015 budget[28] proposes one major change to the child tax credit.[29] Specifically, the budget proposes making the $3,000 refundability threshold permanent (it would not be indexed for inflation). The Treasury Department estimates that this change would reduce revenue by $64.9 billion between 2015 and 2024.

---

[26] For more information, see Len Burman, Elaine Maag, and Georgia Ivsin, et al., *Preliminary Analysis of the Family Fairness and Opportunity Tax Reform Act*, Tax Policy Center, March 4, 2014, http://www.urban.org/UploadedPDF/413046-Family-Fairness-and-Opportunity-Tax-Reform-Act.pdf.

[27] The proposal would also disallow the credit to any taxpayers claiming the foreign earned income exclusion.

[28] See the FY2015 Treasury Greenbook at http://www.treasury.gov/resource-center/tax-policy/Pages/general_explanation.aspx for a summary and cost estimates of the President's tax proposals.

[29] The proposal also would extend the EITC due diligence requirements for paid tax preparers to the child tax credit.

Table 3. Key Changes Made by the Camp Proposal to the Child Tax Credit, 2015

Child Tax Credit Parameter	Current Law (In Effect Since 2009)	Proposed Change Under the Camp Tax Reform Proposal (In Effect Beginning in 2015)
Maximum credit per child	$1,000 per child (not indexed for inflation)	$1,500 per child (indexed for inflation using chained CPI)
Maximum credit per non-child dependent	No credit for non-child dependents	$500 (indexed for inflation using chained CPI)
Refundability Threshold	$3,000 between 2015-2017 (not indexed for inflation)	$3,000 between 2015-2017 (not indexed for inflation)
	$10,000 beginning in 2018 (indexed for inflation using CPI)	$0 beginning in 2018 (i.e., refundable credit is calculated on first dollar of earnings)
Refundability Rate	15%	25%
Phase-out Threshold	$75,000 unmarried taxpayers	$413,750 all filers except married joint filers (head of household filing status repealed under proposal)
	$110,000 married joint filer (not indexed for inflation)	$627,500 married joint filers (indexed for inflation using chained CPI)
Phase-out Rate	5%	5%
Offset AMT tax liability	YES	Not Applicable. AMT would be repealed under the Camp proposal.
Qualifying Child Definition		
Age	Under 17 years. See section of report titled "Definition of a Qualifying Child."	Under 18 years
Nationality	Both citizens/nationals and non-citizens. If the child is not a U.S. citizen, they must be a resident of the United States. See section of report titled, "Definition of a Qualifying Child."	Citizens and nationals only
Taxpayer ID to Claim the Refundable Portion of the Credit	Social Security Number (SSN) or Individual Taxpayer Identification Number (ITIN). (The child or non-child dependent must provide either an SSN or ITIN.)	SSN. For married couples, this ID requirement is met if one spouse has an SSN. (The child or non-child dependent must provide either an SSN or ITIN.)

Source: See http://tax.house.gov/ for the draft legislation, JCT documents, and summaries of this tax reform bill.

Note: Under the Camp Proposal, the definition of a non-child dependent is generally unchanged from the current law description of a qualifying relative (IRC Section 152(d)). A qualifying relative under current law must satisfy tests relating to their relationship to the taxpayer (e.g., brother, sister, father, mother), their gross income (under current law, a qualifying relative must have gross income less than the exemption amount, $3,950 in 2014), support from the taxpayer (i.e., the taxpayer provides the qualifying relative with over half of their support), and may not be a qualifying child. In addition, there is no age test for a qualifying relative.

Table 4. Overview of Modifications to the Child Tax Credit Made by Select Legislation Introduced in the 113th Congress

Parameter of the Credit	Current Law	H.R. 4935	H.R. 4044	H.R. 769	S. 836	S. 1616	Camp Tax Reform Proposal
Maximum credit per child	$1,000 per child (not indexed for inflation)	$1,000 per child (indexed for inflation)[a]	$2,000 per child for 2014 and 2015 only ($1,000 thereafter) (not indexed for inflation)	$1,000 per child (indexed for inflation)[b]	$1,000 per child (indexed for inflation)[c]	$3,500 per child comprised of the current $1,000 per child credit and an "additional refundable credit for children" (ARCC) of $2,500 per child. (The ARCC would be adjusted for inflation)[d]	$1,500 per child (indexed for inflation)
Refundability Threshold	$3,000 between 2015-2017 (not indexed for inflation) $10,000 beginning in 2018 (indexed for inflation using CPI)	same as current law	same as current law	$3,000 (i.e., ARRA modification would be permanent) (not indexed for inflation)	$3,000 (i.e., ARRA modification would be permanent) (not indexed for inflation)	The $1,000 credit refundability threshold is unchanged from current law. The $2,500 ARCC is refundable using an alternative formula.[e]	$3,000 between 2015-2017 (not indexed for inflation) $0 beginning in 2018 (i.e., refundable credit is calculated on first dollar of earnings)
Refundability Rate	15%	same as current law	30% for 2014 and 2015 (15% thereafter)	same as current law	same as current law	The $1,000 credit refundability rate is unchanged from current law. The $2,500 ARCC is refundable using an alternative formula.[e]	25%

Parameter of the Credit	Current Law	H.R. 4935	H.R. 4044	H.R. 769	S. 836	S. 1616	Camp Tax Reform Proposal
Phase-out Threshold	$75,000 unmarried taxpayer $110,000 married joint filer *(not indexed for inflation)*	$75,000 unmarried taxpayer $150,000 married joint filer (twice the level for unmarried taxpayers) *(indexed for inflation)*[a]	same as current law	same as current law	same as current law	The $1,000 credit phases out using the same formula as current law. The $2,500 ARCC does not phase out.	$413,750 other filers, excluding married joint filers (head of household filing status repealed under proposal) $627,500 married joint filers (indexed for inflation using chained CPI)
Phase-out Rate	5%	same as current law	same as current law	same as current law	same as current law	The $1,000 credit phases out using the same formula as current law. The $2,500 ARCC does not phase out.	same as current law

Source: IRC §24, H.R. 4935, H.R. 4044, H.R. 769, S. 836, S. 1616, and the Camp tax reform proposal. See http://tax.house.gov/ for the draft legislation, JCT documents, and summaries of this tax reform bill.

a. The inflation indexing under this bill would occur for inflation occurring after 2014. In 2015, the cost of living adjustment for both the thresholds and the credit amount would be calculated as the ratio of the consumer price index (CPI) in 2014 divided by the CPI in 2013. The credit amount would be rounded to the nearest multiple of $50 and the thresholds would be rounded to the nearest multiple of $1,000.

b. The inflation indexing under this bill would occur for inflation occurring after 2013. In 2015, the cost of living adjustment for the credit amount would be calculated as the ratio of the CPI in 2014 divided by the CPI in 2012. The credit amount would be rounded to the nearest multiple of $50.

c. The inflation indexing under this bill would occur for inflation occurring after 2012. In 2015, the cost of living adjustment for the credit amount would be calculated as the ratio of the CPI in 2014 divided by the CPI in 2011. The credit amount would be rounded to the nearest multiple of $50.

d. The inflation adjustment of the additional refundable credit under Senator Lee's bill would be adjusted for inflation beginning in 2014. The inflation adjustment would be the ratio of the national average wage index for the preceding year divided by the national average wage index for 2012. The credit amount would be rounded to the next lowest multiple of $50.

e. The refundable portion of the ARCC is calculated as the amount by which a taxpayer's individual income and payroll taxes (both the employer and employee portions) exceed the taxpayer's EITC. Hence, the maximum refundable portion of the ARCC would therefore equal 15.3% of earnings minus the refundable portion of the EITC.

Legislation That Modifies the Credit Identification Requirements

When a taxpayer files their income tax return they must provide a unique identification (ID) number. Generally, a taxpayer's ID number is his or her Social Security number (SSN). For those individuals who are not eligible to receive an SSN, they are issued an individual taxpayer identification number (ITIN) by the IRS.[30] ITINs are issued to individuals for the sole purpose of filing tax returns, paying taxes, and otherwise complying with federal tax laws.[31]

For most tax provisions, the tax code does not distinguish between tax filers who use SSNs and those who use ITINs. However, currently one tax provision—the earned income tax credit (EITC)—does include explicit language requiring taxpayers to provide their SSNs[32] in order to be eligible for the credit (hence ITIN filers may not claim the EITC).[33]

There have been a variety of legislative proposals introduced in the 113th Congress to amend the Internal Revenue Code (IRC) to require taxpayers to provide their SSNs (and in some cases, the SSN of the child for whom they are claiming the credit) to receive the child tax credit (both the refundable and non-refundable portion) or just the refundable portion of the credit (the additional child tax credit or ACTC).

Several of these legislative proposals—H.R. 556, H.R. 3788, H.R. 3885, H.R. 1674, S. 18, and S. 1869—would modify the credit's ID requirements such that for a taxpayer to claim the refundable portion of the child tax credit, the taxpayer would need to provide an SSN. In the case of married taxpayers filing jointly, this requirement would be met if either spouse provided an SSN. Two other bills—H.R. 2778 and S. 91—would also require taxpayers to provide SSNs, but in this case the ID requirement would apply to the entire credit, not just the refundable portion. (It is currently unclear in the case of a joint return whether either or both spouses would need to provide their SSNs in order to claim the credit.) Finally, S.Amdt. 2732 to S. 1963 would require taxpayers wishing to claim the refundable portion of the credit to provide the qualifying child's SSN. Unlike other legislation introduced in the 113th Congress, the ID requirements for the taxpayer (and their spouse) would be unchanged by this amendment.

---

[30] For more information on ITINs, see http://www.irs.gov/individuals/article/0,,id=222209,00 html.

[31] For more information, see CRS Report WSLG823, *Social Security Number or Individual Taxpayer Identification Number for Tax Credit? That is the Question*, by Emily M. Lanza, Erika K. Lunder, and Kathleen S. Swendiman.

[32] This statutory language requires that taxpayers provide SSNs associated with work authorization for themselves, their spouses if filing a joint return, and any qualifying children. For more information on "work-authorized" SSNs, see CRS Report WSLG823, *Social Security Number or Individual Taxpayer Identification Number for Tax Credit? That is the Question*, by Emily M. Lanza, Erika K. Lunder, and Kathleen S. Swendiman.

[33] For more information, see CRS Report R42628, *Ability of Unauthorized Aliens to Claim Refundable Tax Credits*, by Erika K. Lunder et al.

Table 5. Overview of Changes Made to the Child Tax Credit ID Requirements by Legislation Introduced in the 113th Congress

	Current law	H.R. 556	H.R. 3788 (§2)	H.R. 3885 (§9)	H.R. 1674	H.R. 2778	S. 91	S. 18 (Title 3)	S. 1869	S.Amdt. 2732ᵃ to S. 1963
ID requirement for taxpayer	none	SSN	SSN	SSN	SSNᵃ	SSN (references ID requirement of 2008 Recovery Rebate §6428(h)(2))	SSN (references ID requirement of 2008 Recovery Rebate §6428(h)(2))	SSN	SSN	none
ID requirement for taxpayers in case of joint returns	none	SSN for either spouse	SSN for either spouse	SSN for either spouse	SSN for either spouse	UNCLEAR. SSN may be required for both spouses. Reference to IRC §6428(h)(2 is not clear.	UNCLEAR. SSN may be required for both spouses. Reference to IRC §6428(h)(2 is not clear.	SSN for either spouse	SSN for either spouse	none
ID requirement for qualifying child	SSN or ITINᶜ	same as current law	same as current law	same as current law	same as current law	same as current law	same as current law	same as current law	same as current law	SSN
Applicability of ID Requirement to Child Tax Credit or the Additional Child Tax Credit (ACTC) only	Child Tax Credit (including ACTC)	Additional Child Tax Credit only	Additional Child Tax Credit only	Additional Child Tax Credit only	Additional Child Tax Credit only	Child Tax Credit (including ACTC)	Child Tax Credit (including ACTC)	Additional Child Tax Credit only	Additional Child Tax Credit only	Additional Child Tax Credit only

Source: IRC §24, H.R. 556, H.R. 3788, H.R. 3885, H.R. 1674, H.R. 2778, S. 91, S. 18, S. 1869, and S.Amdt. 2732 to S. 1963.

a.   For the text of the amendment, see http://www.gpo.gov/fdsys/pkg/CREC-2014-02-10/html/CREC-2014-02-10-pt1-PgS855.htm.

b.   The statutory language states that in order to claim the refundable portion of the child tax credit, the taxpayer (or at least one spouse in the case of a married couple filing jointly) must provide their SSN or "otherwise demonstrate that the taxpayer is authorized to be employed in the United States."

c.   Current law states that child tax credit will not be allowed to a taxpayer "unless they include the name and taxpayer identification number of the qualifying child." Taxpayer identification numbers generally include SSNs and ITINs.

Appendix. Legislative History 1991-1999

Before Enactment: The National Commission on Children and the Contract with America

The first child tax credit was enacted in 1997 as part of the Taxpayer Relief Act of 1997 (P.L. 105-34), but it was conceived years earlier and included in several different bills before it ultimately became law. In 1991, the bipartisan National Commission on Children,[34] which was established to provide solutions to a variety of problems facing children, recommended in its final report to the President the creation of a $1,000 refundable child tax credit for all children through age 18. Their proposed credit amount was indexed for inflation. The report cited slow wage growth, the increasing costs of living, and a rising tax burden for the average family as key factors leading to increased financial burdens on families with children.

The report's authors acknowledged that there were provisions in the tax code meant to address the increased financial burden to families that arose from having children, specifically the exemption for dependents. The dependent exemption was intended to provide economic relief to families with children by reducing taxable income by a fixed amount per dependent, and hence reducing tax liability. However, the amount of the exemption was fixed in nominal terms (i.e., not adjusted for inflation) and the commission's report highlighted the fact that its real value had declined considerably since it was established in 1948.[35] The commission argued against simply increasing the amount of the dependent exemption, noting that such a policy would not provide adequate benefit to lower- and middle-income families. Specifically, the commission noted that the dependent exemption, similar to a tax deduction, provided greater monetary benefit to taxpayers with greater taxable income since it was proportional to a taxpayer's highest marginal tax bracket. And since the dependent exemption could not lower the tax liability of taxpayers who, due to low income, owed no federal income tax, it was unavailable to many families with children who the commission believed most needed economic assistance.

Three years later, in 1994, a child tax credit was included in legislation meant to enact key principles of the Contract with America, a list of policy proposals released by the Republican Party before the 1994 midterm elections. In the 104th Congress, both the American Dream Restoration Act (H.R. 6) and later the Tax Fairness and Deficit Reduction Act of 1995 (H.R. 1215) included a $500 per child nonrefundable[36] tax credit for children under 18 years. The credit began to phase out for families with AGI above $200,000 (regardless of filing status). In response

---

[34] For more information on the National Commission on Children, see their final report: National Commission on Children, *Beyond Rhetoric: A New American Agenda for Children and Families*, Washington, DC, 1991.

[35] In the Joint Committee on Taxation's explanation of the Taxpayer Relief Act of 1997, the committee cited the decline in the real value of the personal exemption by more than one-third over the prior 50 years as evidence of the tax system's failure to reflect a family's ability to pay. According to JCT, "The Congress believed that the individual income tax structure does not reduce tax liability by enough to reflect a family's reduced ability to pay taxes as family size increases. In part, this is because over the last 50 years the value of the dependent personal exemption has declined in real terms by over one third." For more information see U.S. Congress, Joint Committee on Taxation, JCS-23-97, *General Explanation of Tax Legislation Enacted in 1997*, December 17, 1997, pp. 6-7.

[36] The legislative language of the child tax credit included in H.R. 6 was drafted to create a new refundable credit. While the credit created by H.R. 6 could exceed a taxpayer's income tax liability, it could not exceed the sum of their income and Social Security taxes.

---

to the legislation that had been drafted in Congress, President Clinton proposed his own child tax credit during the 104th Congress in his Middle Class Bill of Rights Tax Relief Act of 1995. Under this proposal, the child tax credit was a $300 per child nonrefundable tax credit for tax years 1996 through 1998, increasing to $500 per child after 1998, with income phase-outs beginning at $60,000. The credit amounts were indexed for inflation. An eligible child was defined as being under 13 years of age.[37] President Clinton's proposal was estimated by the Treasury Department to cost $35.6 billion over five years, while the American Dream Restoration Act was estimated to cost $107 billion over the same time period.[38]

Taxpayer Relief Act of 1997 and Other Legislation

After failing to come to an agreement in 1995, Congress and President Clinton revisited the topic of a child tax credit in 1997. The House, Senate, and Clinton Administration all proposed a $500 nonrefundable tax credit. A key distinction among the proposals centered on the interaction of the child tax credit with the EITC, which would have an impact on the availability of the child tax credit to lower-income taxpayers.[39] Both the Senate and House legislation proposed applying the nonrefundable child tax credit after the EITC had already reduced tax liability. President Clinton proposed the application of the child tax credit before the application of the EITC. For many low- and moderate-income taxpayers, claiming the EITC before the nonrefundable child tax credit reduced or eliminated their child tax credit. By contrast, claiming the nonrefundable child credit before the EITC allowed the taxpayer to claim the full amount of the child tax credit they were eligible for and did not change the value of their EITC. For example, assume that in 1997 a two-parent, two-child family has $23,000 of income. This family would have an $825 tax liability before the application of credits. They would also be eligible for $1,325 in the EITC and, assuming the child credit was $500 per child, $1,000 of child tax credit. If the EITC was claimed before the child tax credit, this family's tax liability would be reduced to zero and they would receive the remainder of the EITC as a $500 refund. Since they had no tax liability, they could not claim the $1,000 of nonrefundable child tax credit. If, on the other hand, they claimed the child tax credit first, they could claim $825 of the non refundable child tax credit, reducing their tax liability to zero and then claim the full $1,325 of EITC as a refund.[40]

The child tax credit proposals differed in other ways, notably the interaction of the child tax credit with the child and dependent care credit, the age of a qualifying child, and the income phase-out levels and phase-out rates. Given that the child tax credit was part of a broader tax bill that had to meet budget rules, many of the specific details of the provision were likely agreed upon after evaluating their budgetary impact.

What emerged from the conference negotiations that year was the Taxpayer Relief Act of 1997

---

[37] U.S. Congress, Joint Committee on Taxation, *Background and Information Relating to Three Tax Cut Proposals for Middle Income Americans: A $500 per Child Tax Credit, A Reduction in the Marriage Penalty, and A Deduction for Education and Job Training Expenses.* 104th Cong., 1st sess., March 15, 1995, p. 5.

[38] "Treasury Release Contrasting Revenue Costs of Clinton, GOP Tax Cuts," *Tax Notes Today*, LB1290, December 16, 1994.

[39] For more information on the differences in the House, Senate and Clinton Administration proposals, see Table 1 in the archived CRS Report 97-687E, *Child Tax Credits: Comparison of Proposals for Low-Income Taxpayers*, by Gregg Esenwein and Jack Taylor, available by request.

[40] All these figures are from Table 2 of the archived CRS Report 97-687E, *Child Tax Credits: Comparison of Proposals for Low-Income Taxpayers*, by Gregg Esenwein and Jack Taylor, available by request.

(P.L. 105-34), which established a child tax credit. The credit was structured as a $500 nonrefundable tax credit ($400 in 1998) for most families with qualifying children under 17. The credit phased out at a rate of $50 for every $1,000 by which a taxpayer's modified AGI exceeded thresholds based on filing status, namely $110,000 for taxpayers filing as married joint, $75,000 for taxpayers filing as head of household, and $55,000 for taxpayers filing as married separate. The credit was refundable for taxpayers with three or more qualifying children and was calculated as the excess of a taxpayer's payroll taxes over their EITC (the alternative formula). Neither the credit amount nor the phase-out thresholds were indexed for inflation. The refundable portion of the credit was reduced by the amount of the taxpayer's alternative minimum tax (AMT).[41] In addition, the total amount by which personal nonrefundable credits (including the child tax credit) could reduce an individual's regular tax liability was limited.[42]

The Omnibus Consolidated and Emergency Supplemental Appropriations Act of 1998 (P.L. 105-277), which was enacted shortly after the enactment of the Taxpayer Relief Act of 1997, repealed the provision that reduced the refundable portion of the child tax credit by the AMT for tax year 1998. In addition, this act allowed personal nonrefundable credits (including the child tax credit) to fully offset a taxpayer's regular income tax liability in 1998.[43]

The Ticket to Work and Work Incentives Improvement Act of 1999 (P.L. 106-170) extended the provision in P.L. 105-277 which allowed the nonrefundable personal credit to fully offset regular tax liability for one additional year, through the end of 1999. In addition, for tax years 2000 and 2001, the act included a provision which allowed taxpayers to use their personal nonrefundable credits (including the child tax credit) to not only offset their regular tax liability in full, but also their AMT. Finally, the act also extended for tax years 1999 through 2001 the prior-law repeal of the provision that reduced the refundable portion of the child tax credit by the AMT.

Author Contact Information

Margot L. Crandall-Hollick
Analyst in Public Finance
mcrandallhollick@crs.loc.gov, 7-7582

---

[41] For more information on the AMT, see CRS Report RL30149, *The Alternative Minimum Tax for Individuals*, by Steven Maguire.

[42] The total amount of personal nonrefundable credits was limited to the extent that a taxpayer's regular tax liability exceeded their tentative minimum tax. The tentative minimum tax is an alternative tax calculated using a different definition of taxable income and different tax rates. For more information on the interaction of personal tax credits and the AMT, see CRS Report RL30149, *The Alternative Minimum Tax for Individuals*, by Steven Maguire.

[43] While personal nonrefundable credits could now offset both the regular tax and tentative minimum tax, they could only offset the tentative minimum tax by an amount less than or equal to their regular tax liability. Hence these credits could not offset the AMT (which is defined as the difference between the tentative minimum and regular tax liability). For more information on the interaction of personal tax credits and the AMT, see CRS Report RL30149, *The Alternative Minimum Tax for Individuals*, by Steven Maguire.